Scriptures Come Alive

Grace Bradford

Scriptures Come Alive

Copyright © 1995 by Abingdon Press

This book is printed on acid-free, recycled paper.

ISBN 0-687-00560-4

95 96 97 98 99 00 01 02 03 04 — 10 9 8 7 6 5 4 3 2 1

SCRIPTURES COME ALIVE

SCRIPTURES COME ALIVE

BY GRACE BRADFORD

INTRODUCTION

How often I have sat in worship services in various churches reverently attentive until the scripture lessons were read. "The angel said . . ." "The Pharaoh said . . ." "Moses struck the rock and water gushed forth. . . ." were passages of scripture read by the liturgist all in the same tone of voice. My mind flashed in to the readings occasionally and back out to plan the next day's agenda, the evening's dinner menu or the best time to put the car in the shop.

I decided to make scripture come alive in my church, for I discovered that I was not the only one who too often couldn't remember what the lesson was about.

SCRIPTURES COME ALIVE is to be used by ministers, worship leaders and youth leaders for dreamers like myself who slip away easily, children who become restless during the worship service, teens who need action both in their passive and active involvement and laity of all ages who need to be and should be a part of the worship services. It is designed to bring scripture directly off the pages into the hearts so that one gets the feeling, "He was speaking to me."

CHANCEL DRAMA

Today's technology addresses all of the senses. Multimedia, computerized and live presentations enable us to focus and extend our span of attention and concentration. The word of God is too important to be missed, therefore we in the church must make every effort to make scripture come alive in the minds and hearts of the people

All of the presentations in this collection can be delivered by adults of all ages, children, youth or a combination of all unless indicated. Although each is short in length and intended for delivery in the chancel area of the sanctuary, it can also be used for Sunday School programs, family night or other devotional or social activities.

All presentations have been paraphrased or quoted from the Living Bible or the New Revised Version.

REQUIREMENTS FOR EFFECTIVE PRESENTATIONS

1. Select speakers who can project clearly and who will be available for rehearsals.
2. Presentations need to be read and discussed and unfamiliar words defined so that the speakers will understand what they are saying and will be able to capture the spirit of the presentation.
3. All parts except that of the narrator should be memorized. However, if this is not possible, speakers should become so familiar with lines that they can look up most of the time and look down occasionally.
4. Several rehearsals are necessary so that emphasis can be placed on listening and responding to each other naturally.
5. Scenery is not recommended for use in the chancel area. Necessary furniture and props should be used only if recommended in the script and kept simple. Props should be used in a meaningful way, that is, if palms are to be waved, the waving must be rehearsed in order that it appear spontaneous and natural. Actors, particularly children, need to be comfortable and familiar with their settings and movements of the body.
6. Costumes are not essential to the understanding of the scripture being delivered, but can be used if kept simple (draped and pinned material is sufficient).
7. The director must be able to demonstrate the expression called for in speech and action. Speakers should not be asked to do anything the director cannot demonstrate.
8. Specific hymns to be sung by speakers and congregation as a part of the presentations are often recommended. However, related hymns can be substituted. New hymns or speaking lines for the congregation should be explained and rehearsed during the gathering period so that the flow between performers and congregation and between dialogue and songs will be smooth.
9. Although the congregation assists in the singing, the casts needs to be familiar with the hymns and lead the singing.
10. When small children are participating, they need only to learn the hymn refrain.
11. The director is at liberty to make copies of the script for the speakers and make adjustments in the script to fit the needs of the group.
12. Always, the focus of the congregation and speakers should be on the story being delivered and the message that flows out of it.
13. Speech choir parts may be done by individual persons.
14. Speech choirs 1 and 2 should be grouped according to range of voices, high voices in one group, low voices in the other. Speech choir

groups should speak together, pause together, give same emphasis and inflection in voices, speak slowly and clearly and use hand movements and facial expression as needed.

READING SCRIPTURE ALOUD

Perhaps the most important aspect of the Sunday worship service is the reading of scripture, for so many parts of the service flow out of the scripture lesson—the sermon, the children's message, the hymns and even the anthems. When the readings are based on the Lectionary, three or four readings may be included—an Old Testament lesson, a Psalm, an Epistle lesson and a Gospel lesson. One of these usually becomes the basis of the service.

Scripture lessons are often historical accounts, stories that can be enacted, letters that can be read as monologues, or Psalms that can be sung. Many can be acted out as a drama but all can be read with interest and expression.

Preparation for reading scripture is as necessary as choir rehearsals are for preparing the anthem. Choosing a reader is as important as choosing a soloist. The reader should be able to read loud and clear. Even if a microphone is used, the reader is required to project the voice. The reader must be familiar with the text, understand all of the words and the meaning of each sentence and be able to convey it like it is his own story. The reader must be able to look up and speak, look down and take in a phrase and then look up and say it. Quotation marks indicate conversation, so those passages must be read like conversation. Above all, speak slowly. The listeners need time to listen, hear and decode what is being said.

All scripture passages have words or phrases that should be emphasized. Reading can often come alive simply by using some of the following methods of expression:

1. loud vs. soft passages
2. rapid reading vs. slow drawn out phrases
3. use of the high, medium and low ranges of the voice
4. open and prolonged vowels
5. emphasis on beginning consonants
6. memorization and looking at congregation
7. reading and looking down
8. smiling, frowning and use of other facial expressions
9. use of hands
10. forward or erect movement of the body
11. singing or chanting a line
12. a pause

The passage below will show the use of several of the methods of expression listed above:

1ST CORINTHIANS 13:1-7

If I *speak* in the tongues of mortals and of angels, but do not have love **(pause)**, I am a noisy gong or a clanging cymbal. And if I have prophetic powers and understand all mysteries and all knowledge,and if I have all faith, so as to remove mountains **(rapid)**, but do - not - have - *love* **(pause)**, *I AM NOTHING* **(slow and drawn out)**. If I give away all my possessions, and if I hand over my body **(use hands)** so that I may boast but do not have *love, (pause, look up and speak slow, pointing to self) I - GAIN - NOTHING!*

(Memorize this paragraph) Love is patient; love is kind **(smile)**; love is not envious or boastful or arrogant or rude **(fast)**. It does not insist on its own way; it is not irritable or resentful; it does not rejoice in wrongdoing, *but rejoices in the truth.* **(slow and drawn out)** It *b e a r s* all things, *b e l i e v e s* all things, *h o p e s* all things, *e n d u r e s* **(softly with energy)** all things. (NRSV)

PEOPLE BE JOYFUL

Speech choir

(Present with three speakers or three groups of speakers facing left, center and right sides of congregation.
SPEAKERS enter clapping, shaking tambourines and bells and clashing cymbals.)

ALL: Make a joyful noise to the Lord, people!
Sing to him your songs of Praise.
Strum your guitars and fiddles
Blow your saxophones and trumpets,
Play your handbells and synthesizers.
Beat your drums and shake your tambourines.
Obey the Lord and come before him singing.

GROUP 1:   Hallelujah!

GROUP 2:   Praise ye the Lord!

GROUP 3:   Thanks be to God!

GROUP 1:   For God is good!

GROUP 2:   God made us!

GROUP 3:   We are his children!

ALL: Come into this place with thanksgiving
Then go into the world with praise,
And bless his name,
For God is always good, loving and kind,
And his faithfulness to us will never end.

GROUP 1:   So stand and be joyful! *(motion congregation to stand)*

GROUP 2:   Clap your hands, *(SPEAKERS CLAP HANDS)*

GROUP 3:   Shout with praise!

ALL: God is good! *(Go among people)* God is good! God is good!

(CONGREGATION sings "Praise God, from Whom all Blessings Flow" Lasst uns Erfreuen. Musicians accompany on handbells, trumpets or other instruments)

BREAD AND WATER FROM GOD

Exodus 16, 17:1-7

(Soloist sings hymn: "Marching to Zion", verse 1 as SPEECH CHOIRS take their places on each side of chancel, facing CONGREGATION with MOSES in center.)

NARRATOR: We left Elim and journeyed on into the Sihn Wilderness between Elim and Mt. Sinai, arriving there on the fifteenth day of the second month after leaving Egypt.

PEOPLE 1: Oh, why did we leave Egypt? God could have killed us there just as easily as bringing us out here to die. There is no food. We are dying of starvation.

PEOPLE 2: Are you with us, God or against us?

MOSES: Father, you brought us through the Red Sea making its water stand like great walls so we could pass through, you let down the waters on the chariots and armies of Pharaoh and drowned them at sea. You moved us forward. You sweetened the bitter waters at Marah so we could drink it. Now we are here in this foreign land where there is nothing to eat. My people are starving. What shall I do?

NARRATOR: God told Moses to tell the people he would rain down food from heaven for them to eat it in the morning and flesh to eat in the evening.

PEOPLE 1: This is all nonsense. Even God cannot make bread fall down from the skies. This is a trick of Moses and Aaron. *(PEOPLE 1 turn their backs to congregation)*

PEOPLE 2: There is no meat in these parts for us to eat. If there were we would have found it ourselves. This is the punishment of God. *(PEOPLE 2 turn their backs)*

PEOPLE 1: *(turning toward congregation)* What is this falling around us? It is quail. More than enough for all of us. Moses and Aaron did talk to God. Blessed be Moses and Aaron!

PEOPLE 2: *(Turning)* What is this falling from the heavens above? (PEO-

	PLE pick it up and taste it) It is bread! It tastes like honey. God did answer our prayers. Thanks be to God.
MOSES:	This is the food God has given you. Gather enough on the sixth day for the seventh, for the seventh day is the Sabbath, a day of rest and there will be no food for you to gather on that day.
NARRATOR:	The people of Israel continued to eat the manna from heaven every day. *(Cast and congregation sing second verse of "Marching To Zion")*. Now at God's command, they left Sihn dessert going to Rephidim. But when they reached Rephidim there was no water to drink.
PEOPLE 1:	Moses, we cannot stay here. There is no water to drink. You have brought us to this deserted place. Can't you get water for us to drink?
PEOPLE 2:	Why did we ever leave Sihn? Look at our children and cattle. They shall all die. Give us water now!
MOSES:	Why do you quarrel with me? I have no place to get water. Why don't you pray? Complaining will not help us. You should know by now that God is our only hope.
PEOPLE 1:	You talk to God! He does not listen to us. You are the only one who can come face to face with God. Ask him, "Is He with us or not?" *(PEOPLE 1 turn away)*
PEOPLE 2:	Did God bring us out of Egypt, to kill us and our children and livestock with thirst? Tell us! Tell us! *(PEOPLE 2 turn away)* Why?
MOSES:	Lord, *(praying)* what shall I do with these people? Again they are almost ready to stone me. Tell me, what shall I do? Only you can help us now.
NARRATOR:	God said to Moses, "Go on ahead of the people, and take some of the elders of Israel with you; take in your hand the staff with which you struck the Nile, and strike the rock of Hored. I will be standing there in front of you." Moses obeyed the Lord's command. He went ahead with the elders and lifted his staff and struck with force the huge rock. *(MOSES raises an imaginary staff and moves as if striking the rock.)*
PEOPLE 1:	*(Turning)* Look, *(pointing)* water is coming out of the rock! *(Pause)* It is gushing forth. Tell our people to come! There is more than enough water for all to drink.
PEOPLE 2:	*Turning)* Here, taste the water that God has given us. It is cool and delicious. Let us praise God for this gift of water.

MOSES: This place shall be called Massah and Meribah; Massah meaning "tempting Jehovah to slay us" and Meribah meaning "argument and strife". *(Praying)* Father, we complain and doubt you daily but you never leave us alone. We thank you for all of our blessings.

NARRATOR: Let us all say "Thanks be to God for all of our blessings".

NARRATOR, CAST AND CONGREGATION: Thanks be to God for all of our blessings. *(Verse 4 of "Marching To Zion)*

"Now Thank We All Our God" may be substituted for "Marching To Zion"

CALL TO DISCIPLES

Old Testament

CHARACTERS: PANEL MEMBERS—Moderator, Adam, Eve, Noah, Abraham, Sarah, Moses, Miriam and Deborah. All ages of persons can play any part.

PLAYING TIME: 10 Minutes

PROPERTIES: 6 chairs in semi-circle for PANEL MEMBERS, A podium to the side for NARRATOR

COSTUMES: Biblical robes or present day dress is appropriate

NOTE: Memorization of parts is preferred. Congregation's lines should be printed in the program.

MODERATOR: We are here today to talk about the covenant God entered into with the human family. Our panel includes persons who God called into service. Seated before us are Adam and Eve, Noah, Abraham and Sarah, Moses, Miriam and Deborah. We thank you each for being here with us today. Will you please tell our congregation about your call from God and his pledge to you. We'll begin with Adam.

ADAM: *(Stands and steps forward)* God said to me, "Adam, I have given you a garden in which to live. Every plant that is on the face of the earth and every tree with seed in its fruit is yours for food. I have given you a helper as your partner. And I expect the two of you to live in my image and likeness, to rule over the fish, birds, livestock, earth and its creatures, to be fruitful and multiply, to fill the earth and subdue it. But you are not to eat of the tree of the knowledge of good and evil or you shall die." *(EVE joins him)*

EVE: But when he had gone, the serpent said to me, "Eve, you will not die. When you eat of this tree, your eyes will be opened and you will be like God, knowing good and evil." So I ate the fruit. It was good. I gave Adam some. He enjoyed it too. We discovered good but we also discovered evil.

ADAM: And then God called me. "Adam," he said. I didn't answer. "Adam," he called again. "Where are you?" When I couldn't hide any longer, I said "I'm in the garden, Lord. I was afraid because I was naked so I hid." He said, "Have you eaten from the tree that I commanded you not to eat from?" All I could say was, "Yes God, I did." *(THEY slowly return to seats)*.

MODERATOR: So you did not keep your covenant with God, although God kept his covenant with you.
(ADAM AND EVE drop their heads)
Noah, did God call you to do his work?

NOAH: Yes, when God saw that earth was no longer the paradise he had intended, he called to me, "Noah," he said. *(Comes forward)* "I have decided to make an end of all flesh, for the earth is filled with violence. I am going to destroy all life along with the earth." He gave me step by step instructions as to how to build an ark. I didn't understand it all, but I have always tried to be a servant of the Lord because he has been so good to me. When the ark was built, God said, "I am going to bring a flood of waters on the earth and everything on earth will die. But I will establish a covenant with you. You shall come into the ark, your wife, your sons, your sons wives and two of every kind of every living thing, (a male and a female), and you will be the beginning of a new world and never again shall the waters become a flood to destroy humankind." This is the covenant God made with me and every living creature for all future generations. *(HE sits)*

MODERATOR: Abraham, did God call you? *(ABRAHAM steps forward)*

ABRAHAM: Ten times he called me. The first time he said, "Abraham, leave your country, your people and your father's household and go to the land I will show you. I will make you into a great nation and I will bless you; I will make your name great, and you will be a blessing. I will bless those who bless you, and whoever curses you I will curse; and all peoples on earth will be blessed through you."

MODERATOR: What did you answer?

ABRAHAM: I just went. One does not question or refuse God. I knew that he would do what he promised. I had only to do his will.

SARAH: I remember when Abraham was 100 years old and I was 90, God promised us a child. *(She joins him)* Can you imagine that? We laughed for we could not believe that at my age I could have a child. But I did and God has continued to bless our lives and our children since, just as he said he would if we were faithful. *(They take seats)*

MODERATOR: Moses did God make a covenant with you?

MOSES: Yes, he called me through flames of fire from a burning bush. "Moses, Moses!" he called. It frightened me but I answered, *(standing)* "Here I am, Lord!" God said, "Take off your sandals for the place where you are standing is holy ground. I am the God of your father, the God of Abraham, the God of Isaac and the God of Jacob." Then he told me to lead the Israelites out of Egypt. I said, "Who am I, that I should go to Pharaoh and bring the Israelites out of Egypt? Suppose I go to the Israelites and say to them, 'The God of your fathers has sent me to you,' and they say, 'What's his name?' What shall I tell them? What if they do not believe me or listen to me and say, 'The Lord did not appear to you!' "

(MIRIAM stands)

MIRIAM: But God didn't give up on Moses, just as he doesn't give up on any of us.

Each time Moses pleaded that he was not the one for the mission, he still went forward doing what God had commanded and God was there to provide for our needs. When the Pharaoh would not let us out of Egypt, Moses talked to God and God made the river separate and stand up like great walls so that we could get through. When we were in the wilderness, and there was no food, Moses talked to God and God rained manna from heaven, when there was no water to drink, he told Moses to strike a rock and when he did, great streams of water gushed forth. God called Moses to lead his people. Moses did and God was faithful to us all. I know because I was there singing and rejoicing because of God's goodness to us. *(They sit)*

MODERATOR: Deborah, did God call you? *(DEBORAH steps forward)*

DEBORAH: God gave me gifts and talents as he gives to all of you. He trusted me to use them for his people. He gave me the gift of spiritual vision and courage. I was a counselor to my people in the time of peace. But in the time of war, I saw them filled with fear as the enemy's 900 chariots of iron approached. I knew that God would come to our rescue if we honored him. So I called Barak, our leader and together we worked out a plan of action against the enemy. Barak said "If you will go with me into battle. I will go." I was not afraid of the Jabin army or their 900 chariots, for my God who was mightier than Pharaoh, who had brought the Israelites out of Egypt and through the wilderness was mightier than Sisera and his army. We marched forward. Sisera, their leader came with his entire army but God sent a storm of sleet and hail to overcome them. The chariots sank in the mud and Sisera ran for his life but was killed when he went to sleep. I sang then and I continue to sing "Praise the Lord, Israel's leaders bravely led and the people gladly followed! Praise the Lord". *(She returns to her seat.)*

MODERATOR: We have heard from Biblical persons from the past. Members of **(name congregation or gathering)**, I now ask you, "Has God called you? Does he continue to say to you, "Feed my sheep? Have you answered like Abraham, hesitated like Moses or turned away like Adam? What is your answer to God's call?

CONGREGATION: We have heard God's call many times. Sometimes we have answered and sometimes turned away. But he has continually led, guided, protected, forgiven and loved us. We will no longer ignore or run away from him. We will not hesitate or doubt our ability for God has already given us individual talents and made each of us a part of this body of many talents. If we put our faith to the test, God stands ready to give us the strength to carry out the mission. God has assured us that he will never leave us alone.

(CAST and congregation sing hymn: "Jesus Calls Us". This can be followed by hymn: "Here I Am, Lord")

ALL PARTS OF ONE BODY

1st Corinthians 12:12-26

(Four PERSONS face congregation spaced away from each other. After each speaks, each comes closer to center)

PERSON 1: We are all a part of one body, the body of Christ. For just as the body is one and has many members, and all the members of the body, though many, make up one body, so it is with Christ. For in the one spirit we were all baptized into one body and given one faith—faith in Christ.

PERSON 2: The body does not consist of one member but of many. If my foot would say "Because I am not a hand, I do not belong to this body," that would not make it any less a part of my body.

PERSON 3: If my ear would say, "Because I am not an eye, I do not belong to your body," that would not make it any less a part of my body.

PERSON 4: If my whole body were an eye, where would my hearing be?

PERSON 1: If my whole body were an ear, where would my sense of smell be?

PERSON 2: You see God arranged the members in the body, each one of them, as he chose. If all were a single member, where would the whole body be?
(All are together in center)

PERSON 3: In the same way, there are many members in this church, yet one body. The ushers cannot say to the choir, "We have no need of you".

PERSON 4: The adults cannot say to the children, "We don't need you". In fact, the members of the body that seem to be weak, we can't do without.

PERSON 1: And the members of the body who think they are less honorable, we should clothe with great honor.

PERSON 2: And our less respected members should be treated with great respect.

PERSON 3:   God has arranged it this way, so that there will be no differ-
ences in our church, but all of us will care for each other.

ALL: *(Pointing to congregation)* If you suffer, we all suffer. If you are
honored, we all rejoice in the honor.

All sing with congregation the hymn: "One Bread, One Body"

*(Hymns "Christ, from Whom All Blessings Flow" or "They'll Know We Are
Christians By Our Love" may be substituted.)*

GOD'S FAITHFULNESS

Psalm 78

NARRATOR: Listen now to what I tell you, O children of the 21st century. I will tell you a story of things that I have heard and known, that my ancestors told me, that you must tell your children; and we must tell the coming generation so they will not forget God and make the same mistakes as their ancestors.

This story is of the glorious deeds of the Lord, and his might, and the wonders he has done. It is to remind you not to forget the works of God, but to keep his commandments; and not be stubborn and rebellious like your ancestors, whose spirits were not faithful to God. God made a covenant with his people but they refused to walk according to his law. They forgot what he had done for them.

GROUP 1: When they were in bondage in the land of Egypt, God worked marvels in their lives.

He divided the sea like great walls standing on each side and let them pass through.

In the daytime he led the people with a cloud and at night with a fiery light.

He split rocks open in the wilderness and gave them water to drink in abundance.

GROUP 2: *(sadly)* Yet they still sinned against him. They tested him. They spoke against him.

VOICE 1: "We are hungry and thirsty. God can not spread a table in the wilderness. He cannot give us meat and bread to eat."

GROUP 1: Though they had no faith in God and did not trust his saving power, God still commanded the skies above to open and rained down on them manna to eat. Winged birds like the sand of the seas fell within their camp and they ate and were filled. God gave them what they craved.

GROUP 2: But while food was still in their mouths, they sinned.

They did not believe in the wonders of God.

19

	They flattered God with their mouths, but they were lying with their tongues.
VOICE 2:	God grew angry with them and showed his wrath to those who denounced him.
GROUP 1:	But to those who were faithful he bestowed treasures upon them.
GROUP 2:	Over and over they rebelled against him and grieved his heart.
GROUP 1:	But still he led them forth like a flock, guiding them safely through the wilderness.
GROUP 2:	They turned back from entering the Promised Land and erected idols and altars to other gods.
VOICE 2:	When God saw their deeds, his wrath was strong! He routed his enemies and drove them back sending them to eternal shame.
GROUP 1:	But he raised up David from the tribe of Judah, took him from feeding the sheep, made him shepherd over his people where he cared for them with a true heart and skillful hand.
NARRATOR:	And so my brothers and sisters, when you are outraged by injustice, cry out to God, not against him for in times of disaster our trust must remain in God.

(Cast and Congregation sing hymn: "I Will Trust In The Lord")

RIGHTEOUS LIVING

Psalm 26, Micah 1:2, 2:1-18, 2 Timothy 2:19
(Groups 1 & 2 stand on either side of the chancel with backs to congregation)

LEADER: Attention! Let all the peoples of the world listen. For the Lord in his Holy Temple has spoken to me, Micah in a vision and made accusations against you!

Woe to you who lie awake at night, plotting wickedness; you rise at dawn to carry out your schemes; because you can, you do. You want a certain piece of land, or someone else's house (though it is all he has); you take it by fraud and threats and violence.

But the Lord says to you:

VOICE OF GOD: I will reward your evil with evil; nothing can stop me; never again will you be proud and haughty after I am through with you. Your enemies will taunt you and mock your dirge of despair.

GROUP 1: *(Turns to face congregation)* We are finished, ruined. God has confiscated our land and sent us far away, and given what is ours to others.

LEADER: Others will set your boundaries then. The people of the Lord will live where they are sent.

GROUP 1: Don't say such things. Don't harp on things like that. It's disgraceful, that sort of talk. Such evils surely will not come our way.

LEADER: Is that the right reply for you to make, O House of Jacob? Do you think the Spirit of the Lord likes to talk to you so roughly? No! His threats are for your good, to get you on the path again. Yet to this very hour your people rise up and steal the shirts right off the backs of those who trusted them, people who walk in peace.

You have driven out the widows from their homes and stripped their children of every God-given right.

Up! Begone! This is no more your land and home, for you have filled it with sin and it will vomit you out.

21

(Hymn: "Nobody Knows The Trouble I See" is sung by GROUP ONE and congregation. GROUP TWO now turns toward congregation.)

VOICE TWO: Dismiss all the charges against us, Lord, for we have tried to keep your laws and have trusted you without wavering. Cross-examine us, O Lord, and see that this is so; test our motives and affections too. For we have taken your loving kindness and your truth as our ideals.

GROUP TWO: We do not have fellowship with tricky, two-faced people; they are false and hypocritical. We hate the sinners hang-outs and refuse to enter them.

VOICE TWO: We wash our hands to prove our innocence and come before your altar, singing a song of thanksgiving and telling about your miracles.

GROUP TWO: Lord, we love your home, this shrine where the brilliant, daz-zling splendor of your presence lives. Don't treat us as common sinners or murderers who plot against the innocent and demand bribes.

VOICE TWO: No, we are not like that, O Lord; We try to walk a straight and narrow path of doing what is right; therefore in mercy save us and keep us from slipping and falling.

(Hymn: "Lord, I Want To Be A Christian")

ALL: God's truth stands firm like a great rock, and nothing can shake it. It is a foundation stone with these words written on it: "The Lord knows those who are really his," and "A person who calls himself a Christian should not be doing things that are wrong."
(Hymn: "Lord, I Want To Be A Christian" Verse 2)

Hymn: "How Firm A Foundation" may be substituted.

22

DEPENDING ON GOD FOR HELP

A litany for the new year based on Psalm 121

LEADER: As we begin to plan the ministries of this church for this new year, let us lift up our eyes to Jehovah, our God for help and direction, remembering that we can do nothing alone. Our help comes from the Lord who made heaven and earth.

PEOPLE: Though it is often difficult getting people to work on our committees, and plan meaningful ministries, we remind ourselves that when we are committed, God will not let us be hindered from doing his work. The God who controls the heavens, the earth, the seasons and the functions of all living things will neither slumber nor sleep while we toil.

LEADER: The Lord is our keeper, the leader of this church, the planner of our ministries, the commissioner of our time, talents and gifts and is always at our right side protecting us and granting us wisdom and illumination.
The sun, moon nor anything else can strike down the work that we have been chosen to do, for it is God's work and we are all God's children.

PEOPLE: Together we ask the Lord to keep us from all negative thoughts and deeds, to keep his arms around the people in this church and community whom we serve.

ALL: Together, we give thanks to God, in advance, for guiding our going and coming from this time on and throughout the year.

(All sing hymn: "This Is A Day Of New Beginnings".)

MESSAGE FROM THE MOUNT

Matthew 5:1-12
Monologue

WOMAN: I arrived at the hillside just before dawn and already the hillside was filled with people. Some had been there all night. I found a path on the side they had left for him. On both sides of it were people who were blind, lame, diseased, some who couldn't hear and some who were possessed by demons. They just wanted to be near him, to touch the hem of his garment or just to hear him say words of comfort. It wasn't too long after when we saw him. His walk was slow but strong. His disciples were behind him. A crowd followed. I wondered where they would sit but I had seen him feed thousands of people before so I knew he could seat the multitude that was assembling. As he climbed the path, he touched and blessed each one he passed.

When he got to the top, he stood there looking out over the crowd until everyone was seated. Then he smiled and spoke first to those along the path, "Blessed are you who are humble, for the kingdom of Heaven is given to you. Blessed are you who mourn, for you will be comforted. Blessed are you who are meek and lowly, for the whole wide world belongs to you.

Happy are those of you who want to be just and good, for you shall be completely satisfied. Happy are the kind and merciful, for you shall be shown mercy. And you whose hearts are pure, shall be happy for you shall see God. Those among you who strive for peace, will be called the children of God. Those who are persecuted because you are good, will be happy for the Kingdom of Heaven will be yours.

When you are reviled and persecuted and lied about because you are my followers, consider yourselves fortunate. Be very glad, for a tremendous reward awaits you in heaven. And remember, the ancient prophets were persecuted too.

Then he began to move through the crowd touching us gently as he passed. "My children," he said, "You are special to me. You are the world's seasoning, to make it tolerable. If you lose your flavor, what will happen to the world? And what will happen to you? You will be considered worthless and will be trampled underfoot. You are the world's light–like a city on a hill, glowing in the night for all to see. Don't ever hide your light. Let it shine for all; let your good deeds glow for all to see, so that they will praise your heavenly Father."

He stayed and talked until almost dusk, then he bowed his head, prayed quietly and left. I sat there entranced until he was out of sight, then I started home trying to remember all he had said. One thing that stayed with me throughout the evening, and still remains foremost in my heart, I'll share with you. He said, "You are the world's light, a city on a hill glowing in the night for all to see. Don't ever hide your light. Let is shine. Let your good deeds glow for all to see, so that they will praise your heavenly Father."

(SPEAKER or congregation will sing hymn: "This Little Light Of Mine")

I REMEMBER JESUS

Cast - 12 persons of different ages

(PERSONS 1-6 gather together in chancel area casually exchanging their recollections of Jesus. They respond with words of agreement and exclamation after each speaker)

PERSON 1:   It's been a while now, almost a year and yet we keep going over it in our minds, reminding each other that it did happen and he was here. Some folks want to act as if it never happened, or as if it ended when he died. But we know better. Actually it just began when he died. We're beginning to understand better and even though he's not here in the flesh, everyday we witness his miracles. He's still working with us and all around us. We come together whenever we can and wherever we can to celebrate his victory over death and we're glad you came today. For your being here lets us know you have a story to tell too. It's never formal here. We just testify and sing and pray and praise him. Wherever we go, we tell the story. Help us tell it.

(Hymn: "We've a Story to Tell to the Nations")

PERSON 2:   There's a story I tell wherever I go. There was a young girl in my town who had been sick for so long. She finally died. All of the people who knew her were gathered around the body mourning when Jesus arrived at the house. "Move them out", he said, "and stop the mournful music! Rejoice! She is not dead; she is asleep!" Nobody believed him for they had seen her take her last breath hours before he came. When Jesus stepped into her room, it was like a fresh fragrance filled the air. He lifted her hand and she instantly got up, healed and whole. And she has not been sick since. He raised her from the dead. I know, for I was that girl. *(Group responds)*

PERSON 3:   Well, I saw him passing on his way to the rabbi's house. I had heard about him, but I could never get to him because I had been sick for 12 years. But I knew if I could just touch him, I

26

would be healed. I limped over to him and just as I was about touch him, I fell and all I could do was touch the tassel of his robe. He turned and looked at me and said, "Daughter, all is well. Your faith has healed you." That's all he said. Now, look at me! Look at me! I am well and I praise the Lord!

PERSON 4:   See this hand. It was once deformed and I could not use it at all. I was in the crowd and Jesus found me and said, "Stretch out your arm" and when I did, it became normal. Now I can weave baskets and mold vases and everything I make is to the glory of God. *(Holds up his sculpture)*

PERSON 5:   I was possessed by demons. I was blind and unable to talk. Jesus healed me and now I can see everything—the sky, the birds, the flowers of all colors, and I can speak. I can whisper, "Thanks be to God!" I can sing "How Great Thou Art!" And I can shout for all the world to hear the words of Psalm 150. "Hallelujah! Praise the Lord! Praise him in his temple, and in the heavens. Praise him for his mighty works. Praise him with the trumpet and harp. Let everything alive join me in giving praises to the Lord!"

PERSON 6:   I had been paralyzed for years. I had been to all of the doctors and no one could heal me. My friends heard that Jesus was in town and carried me on my stretcher to see him. Miles they had walked to get to him and when we finally got there it was almost night. There were so many people crowded in the building where he was speaking that we couldn't get near him, so my friends climbed up on the roof and lifted my stretcher to the top and gently let me down in the center of the room where Jesus was. He didn't even have to touch me. He simply said "Cheer up, son. For I have forgiven your sins! Pick up your stretcher and go on home for you are healed."

PERSON 1:   Don't sit so far back in the crowd. Surely you have a story to tell too. Come close so that we can all hear. *(PERSONS 1-6 move back as PERSONS 7-12 move forward as all sing hymn.) Hymn: "Tell Me the Stories of Jesus"*

PERSON 7:   I can't believe I won't see him again. We learned so much from the stories he told us. I remember once when some mothers were bringing their children to Jesus to bless them, the disciples shooed them away, telling them not to bother him. When Jesus saw what was happening, he said, "Let the children come to me, for the Kingdom of God belongs to them. Don't send them away! Take a lesson from them. Any-

27

one who refuses to come to God as a little child will never be allowed into God's Kingdom." And then he gathered the children to him and blessed them.

PERSON 8: One time John said to Jesus, "Teacher, we saw a man using your name to cast out demons. We told him not to, for he was not one of our group." Jesus quickly said to John. "Don't forbid him! For people who do miracles in my name will not quickly turn against me. Anyone who so much as gives you a cup of water because you are Christ's, will be rewarded. But if anyone causes one of these children who believe in me to loose faith, it would be better for that man if a huge millstone were tied around his neck and he were thrown into the sea."

PERSON 9: Do you remember the man who came running to Jesus, knelt down and said, "Good teacher, what must I do to get to heaven"? Remember his answer? He said, "You know the commandments: don't kill, don't commit adultery, don't steal, don't lie, don't cheat, respect your father and mother." The man said, "Oh, I've never broken a single one of those laws." Jesus looked at him with love in his eyes and said, "Then there is one other thing you must do. Go sell all you have and give the money to the poor, and you shall have treasure in heaven, and then come, follow me." The man was stunned. He went sadly away shaking his head, for you see he was very rich. Then Jesus turned to us and said," It is hard for those who put their trust in riches to enter the Kingdom. It is easier for a camel to go through the eye of a needle than for a rich man to enter the Kingdom of God." We looked at each other. We couldn't believe what he was saying. One of the disciples asked him," Then who in the world can be saved, if not a rich man?" "My children," he said to us, "Without God, it is utterly impossible. But with God everything is possible."

PERSON 10: I remember one time James and John were whispering together. Then they went to Jesus and said," Master, when you get to the kingdom, we want to sit on the thrones next to yours, on each side of you. Jesus said "You don't know what you are asking! Are you able to drink from the bitter cup of sorrow I must drink from? Or be baptized with the baptism of suffering I must be baptized with?" They didn't understand what he was saying. None of us did. But they said "Oh, yes, we are!" Jesus said to them, "Then you shall drink from my cup and be baptized with my baptism, but I do not have the right to place you on thrones next to mine. Those appointments have already been made." Then he turned to all of us and said," Whoever wants to be great among you must be a servant. And whoever wants to be greatest of all must be the slave of all. For even I, the Messiah, am not here to be served but to help others, and to give my life as a ransom for many."

PERSON 12: *(from the audience)* Hear me! Hear my story! Jesus gave his life for all of us. He was betrayed, crucified and buried in a tomb. But he arose from the dead, and I still remember the last thing he said before he ascended into heaven to be with God. He said, "Go into all the world and preach the Good News to everyone, everywhere. Tell them what I have taught you. Tell them that God loves them. Make disciples in all the nations, baptizing them in the name of the Father and of the Son and of the Holy Spirit, and then teach these new disciples to obey all the commandments.

ALL: Christ is with us always, even to the end of the world!

PERSON 1: Your stories are wonderful and there are many more of them. I can see on your faces *(To audience)* you have one, you have one, and you. But it is growing late and we must be starting home. But go into the world and tell your stories, all of you. Let everyone know that Jesus Christ is still with us!

(CAST sings refrain of "Go Tell it on the Mountain" as they take their seats)

A HOMECOMING

Luke 15:11-32

(Costumes are appropriate. Chancel steps or a bench may be used by SON. VOICES may be done by individuals or 3 speech choirs)

STORYTELLER: There was once a man, very wealthy with a big house, lots of land and many servants working for him, gathering the crops and caring for his farm animals. He had two sons who worked hard helping to care for the estate. One day the youngest son came to him.

SON: Father I wish to have a word with you. It is time for me to go out and explore the world. Give me my share of the property now, there are things I wish to do.

FATHER: Your share? Your share? A child does not receive inheritance until after the death of his parents. How dare you ask me for your inheritance. *(FATHER turns away from his SON and bows his head.)* Oh God, our help in ages past, our hope for years to come, grant me your patience, your wisdom and your love. *(Pause)*
(FATHER turns back to his SON) Here, my son. Take this. It is your share of the inheritance. The Lord bless you and give his angels charge over you.

(Hymn: "Gift of Love", verse one is sung by soloist or congregation. the SON Exits in one direction and enters from another.)

STORYTELLER: The son had all good intentions but the temptations surrounding him were very great. *(VOICES OF TEMPTATION meet him in the center).*

VOICE ONE: Come stranger. Let us welcome you to this new country. *(SON stops to listen to voices, tries to leave but gives in to their attention).*

VOICE TWO: You dress well. You must be wealthy. Let us help you have a good time.

VOICE THREE: There are many places to go and much to do. Enjoy yourself. Spend your money freely like the rest of us are doing.

30

VOICE ONE:	We can eat and drink lavishly and even gamble a little.
VOICE TWO:	Why work when you can have fun. Leave the work for the poor people. Life is meant to be enjoyed when you have money.
VOICE THREE:	We will introduce you to new pleasures.
VOICE ONE:	Don't hesitate. Life is too short to waste time deciding what to do. I know just the place where you can get a new robe fit for a king. Take this one off. Let me check it for size.
VOICE TWO:	Come on, spend your time with friends. Spend your money on your new friends. If you look after us, we'll look after you.
VOICE THREE:	Spend your life! Spend your life!
ALL:	Spend! Spend! Spend! *(They gather around him removing his robe and urging him to go with them. They quickly exit with the robe. The SON moves around aimlessly and then drops to his knees.)*
STORYTELLER:	And he did spend until all of his money was gone. When he had spent everything, a great famine arose in that country. Now a famine is when there is not enough food and the people are starving. The son was starving. he had nothing to eat and no more money to spend. Finally one of the citizens gave him a job feeding the pigs and hogs. *(SON moves around on hands and knees pantomiming feeding the pigs. VOICES OF CONDEMNATION enter.)*
VOICE ONE:	Look at the stranger. He is a pig herder. *(They laugh and make fun of him.)*
VOICE TWO:	Pigs and hogs are unclean animals. That makes him an unclean person.
VOICE THREE:	He is a traitor to Judaism. He cannot practice his religion if he feeds the swine. It is written in the Mishnah, "Cursed be the man who would breed swine. "Cursed be the man!
SON:	Woe is me. I have no money. I have no food to eat. I feed the swine just to have a crust of bread to eat, but still I am hungry. I am tempted to eat the pod that I feed the swine. As bitter as they are, they would be soothing to my mouth and my stomach. But no, this food is repulsive to me and to my people. Look at me, I am repulsive. *(He slumps down on steps or floor and cries.)* My father's hired servants have bread enough to spare while here, I am dying of hunger. *(Pause. He then stands)* I will leave this place and go to my father and I will say to him, "Father, I have sinned against heaven and before

you. I am no longer worthy to be called your son. Treat me as one of your hired servants. *(Hymn: "Gift Of Love" plays as Son circles room, first with head and body bent. As he approaches front center he lifts his head and body.)*

FATHER: Oh God, is it . . . Is it my son? He moves like my son, only slowly and bent and broken. I will go to him. *(FATHER meets SON)* My son . . . my son you have come home!

SON: Father, I have sinned against heaven and before you. I am no longer worthy to be called your son.

FATHER: God has brought you home to me as I asked him to. You are my son and I forgive you. *(Calls out to SERVANTS)* Bring quickly the best robe and put it on him. Put a ring on his hand and shoes on his feet and bring the fatted calf and kill it and let us eat and make merry for this, my son was dead, and is alive again. He was lost and is found.

OLDER SON: *(enters)* Father, what is going on? Brother, you have come back.

FATHER: Come join us, son. Your brother is home and we are going to have a homecoming celebration.

OLDER SON: No, I will not join you! All of these years he has been away, I have served you. I have done all that you have asked of me. I have worked with you in the fields and in the house day after day. I have never disobeyed your command. Yet you never gave me a banquet that I might celebrate with my friends. But when this son of yours comes, who has spent your money recklessly with evil people, you killed for him the fatted calf, not the lamb or the goat, but the fatted calf which is usually prepared only for a wedding or a noble visit from the governor. You are making him a guest of honor.

FATHER: Son, you are always with me and all that I have is yours. Your brother was dead and is now alive; he was lost but now is found. Forgive him and rejoice with me.

OLDER SON: Forgive him! I can't forgive him!

STORYTELLER: For hours he wrestled with his conscience over his brother's return. He asked himself many questions. Should he forgive him! Why should he forgive him! How could he forgive him? His conscience answered him.

VOICE OF CONSCIENCE: Do you love your brother?

OLDER SON: Yes, in certain ways. But this is not about love. It is about worthiness.

VOICE OF CONSCIENCE: No, this is not about worthiness. This is about love and love is forgiving. God grants us his grace whether we are worthy or not because God loves us.

OLDER SON: How do we know that he has truly repented? He may have just come home because he was hungry and penniless. After he gets on his feet, he may leave again. How can we be sure he is going to live right?

VOICE OF CONSCIENCE: God has not made us judge over our sisters and brothers. Jesus said "Do not judge and you will not be judged. Forgive and you will be forgiven".

OLDER SON: How many times must I forgive him?

VOICE OF CONSCIENCE: Jesus said seventy times seven. Lord, we ask you to help us all to forgive.

FATHER: Come my sons, the bells are about to ring out letting the people know that my youngest son, their son has come home. We will go to greet them.

STORYTELLER: And so a joyous celebration was planned and families far and near who had been separated for various reasons came together to be a part of this great homecoming. Let us, in this church reach out and welcome others into our church family.

(ALL sing Hymn: "This Is A Day Of New Beginnings".)

PALM SUNDAY

Matthew 21

(The refrain of hymn, "Mantos y Palmos" is played as the TWO LEADERS take their places on each side of the chancel. Some palms can already be seen in containers placed on the altar. This dialogue takes place just before the passing of the palms. A procession of children await entry.)

LEADER 1: As Jesus and the disciples approached Jerusalem, and were near the town of Bethphage on the Mount of Olives, Jesus sent two of them into the village ahead.

LEADER 2: Jesus said: "Just as you enter you will see a donkey tied there, with its colt beside it. Untie them and bring them here. If anyone asks you what you are doing, just say, " 'The Master needs them' and there will be no trouble."

LEADER 1: This was done to fulfill the ancient prophecy, "Tell Jerusalem her King is coming to her, riding humbly on a donkey's colt!" *(CHILDREN enter singing hymn and waving palms. They proceed to chancel area)* (TLB)

LEADER 1: Who Is this man you have thrown down your coats for.
Who is this man you wave palm branches for?

CHILDREN: It is Jesus of Nazareth! It is King David's son!

LEADER 2: God has given us a King!

CHILDREN: Long live the King! *(They wave palms)*

LEADER 1: Let all heaven rejoice!

CHILDREN: Long live the King! *(They wave palms)*

LEADER 2: Praise God in the highest heaven!

CHILDREN: Long live the King! *(They wave palms)*

LEADER 1&2: Hosanna to the King!

CHILDREN: Long live the king! *(They go into the congregation and pass the palms as the congregation sings.)*

"The Palms" or "Rejoice Ye Pure In Heart" may be substituted for
"Mantos y Palmos"

MAUNDY THURSDAY

John 13

(This dialogue is placed in the service just before the foot washing. SPEAKERS come to the chancel as a hymn is sung. NARRATOR stands at the podium. JESUS AND PETER face each other.)

NARRATOR: Jesus knew on the evening of Passover Day that it would be his last night on earth before returning to his Father. During supper, the devil had already suggested to Judas Iscariot, Simon's son, that this was the night to carry out his plan to betray Jesus. Jesus knew that the Father had given him every-thing and that he had come from God and would return to God. So he got up from the supper table, took off his robe, wrapped a towel around his loins, poured water into a basin, and began to wash the disciples feet and to wipe them with the towel he had around him. Then he came to Simon Peter.

PETER: Master, you shouldn't be washing our feet like this!

JESUS: You don't understand now why I am doing it; but some day you will.

PETER: No, you shall never wash my feet!

JESUS: But if I don't, you can't be one of my people.

PETER: Then wash my hands and head as well—not just my feet!

JESUS: One who has bathed all over needs only to have his feet washed to be entirely clean. Now you are clean.

NARRATOR: After washing their feet Jesus put on his robe again and sat down and asked them as he now asks us:

JESUS: *(To PETER and CONGREGATION)* Do you understand what I was doing? You call me 'Master' and 'Lord' and you do well to say it, for it is true. And since I, the Lord and Teacher, have washed your feet, you ought to wash each other's feet. I have given you an example to follow: do as I have done to you. How true it is that a servant is not greater than his master. Nor is the messenger more important than the one who sends him. You know these things—now do them! That is the path of blessing. (TLB)

(Liturgical dancers or two youth bring forward the basin and pitcher of water, and place them on a table in the chancel area as choir sings "Jesu, Jesu".)

GOOD FRIDAY

John 18:29–19:16

To be presented at the beginning of the Good Friday service

(PILATE and JESUS stand in center. CROWD stands facing PILATE and JESUS with backs to the congregation. CONGREGATION can function as the CROWD. Soloist passes through chancel area singing one verse of "Were You There?")

PILATE:	You have brought this man to me. What are you accusing him of?
CROWD:	He's a criminal!
PILATE:	Then take him away and judge him yourselves by your own laws.
CROWD:	But we want him crucified, and we need your approval.
PILATE:	*(Turns to JESUS)* Are you the King of the Jews?
JESUS:	'King' as you use the word or as the Jews use it?
PILATE:	I'm not a Jew. Your own people and their chief priests brought you here. Why? What have you done? Answer me? Are you a king?
JESUS:	I'm not an earthly king. If I were, my followers would have fought for me when I was arrested by the Jewish leaders. But my Kingdom is not of this world.
PILATE:	But you are a King then?
JESUS:	Yes, I was born for that purpose. And I came to bring truth to the world. All who love truth are my followers.
PILATE:	*(Irritated)* What is this truth? *(Turns to crowd)* I have questioned him. Though I do not understand his answers, I cannot find him guilty of any crime. You have a custom of asking me to release someone from prison each year at Passover. So if you want me to, I'll release the "King of the Jews".
CROWD:	*(Screaming)* No! Not this man. Release Barabbas.
PILATE:	But Barabbas is a robber. This man has committed no such crime. I am going to release him now, but understand clearly

	that I find him not guilty.
CROWD:	No! Crucify him! Crucify! Crucify!
PILATE:	You crucify him! I find him not guilty!
CROWD:	By our laws he ought to die because he calls himself the Son of God.
PILATE:	*(To JESUS)* You hear the accusation. Do you have anything to say? *(Pause)* Don't you realize that I have the power to release you or to crucify you?
JESUS:	You have no power over me unless it is given to you by God. Those who brought me to you have the greater sin.
CROWD:	If you release this man, you are no friend of Caesar's. Anyone who declares himself a king is a rebel against Caesar.
PILATE:	Then I give him to you. Here is your king!
CROWD:	Away with him! Away with him! Crucify him!
PILATE:	What? Crucify your king?
CROWD:	We have no king but Caesar! We have no king but Caesar!
PILATE:	Take him and do what you will do! *(He turns his back to them. All others freeze. Soloist re-enters singing second verse of "Were You There?")*

To be spoken at the conclusion of the Good Friday service

(JOSEPH:	(TO CONGREGATION) I am Joseph, a member of the Jewish Supreme Court, from the city of Arimathea in Judea. I do not understand the actions of my fellow leaders. I had long been expecting the Messiah's coming. It had been prophesied. I do not want my king to remain there on the cross. May I have the body? I will wrap it in linen and take it to a new, unused tomb in the rock on the side of the hill. His friends here Galilee will go with me. May I have the body?
	(Chancel area is stripped of paraments, as congregation sings 3rd verse "Were You There?" unaccompanied. Congregation leaves in silence.)

HE AROSE

An Easter Sunday Pageant

Scenes 1 and 2 may be used separately or as a skit. Simple costumes will enhance the presentation.

(As quiet music is played, speakers take their places in the chancel area. The angel and Jesus are placed stage left and right, respectively behind palms so that their visibility is not clear.)

NARRATOR: It was early on Sunday morning when Mary Magdalene, Joanna and Mary the mother of James went to the tomb taking ointments. They found that the huge stone covering the entrance had been rolled aside.

MARY: *(Turning toward the two ladies with her)* Look! The stone has been rolled away. Someone has been here.

MARY M: The tomb is empty! Jesus! Where is he?

JOANNA: They've taken him away. We should have stayed with him. We knew we should have stayed here.

MARY: The soldiers! They stole my Lord! Oh! Where did they take him?

JOANNA: There's the burial cloth he was wrapped in and the swathe that covered his head is lying over there.

MARY M: Go and find Peter. Tell him to come at once!

(ANGEL appears at left and startles the women)

ANGEL 1: Don't be startled. I know you are looking for Jesus, who was crucified, but he isn't here. He has come back to life again, just as he said he would. Go quickly and tell the disciples that he has risen from the dead, and that he is going to Galilee to meet them there. *(ANGEL returns to unseen position)*

JOANNA: You mean he's alive. But how?

MARY: Jesus is alive. This is such good news. John and the others will be so happy to know that Jesus is alive. Come, we must not let the guards know.

(They turn to leave)

JESUS:	*(Appears stage right)* Good morning!
WOMEN:	Jesus! You are alive. Let me touch you! *(LADIES fall to the ground. Mary M. tries to touch him.)*
JESUS:	Do not touch me. I have not yet ascended to the Father, But go find my brothers and tell them that I soon shall ascend to my God and your God. Tell them to meet me in Galilee.

(Congregation and cast sing, "Christ The Lord is Risen Today")

THE WALK TO EMMAEUS

This may be used as SCENE TWO of "He Arose" or as a separate presentation.

(TWO DISCIPLES enter from left of chancel talking together and stop at center.)

DISCIPLE 1:   It is so hard to believe. He had been with us so long. We were learning so much from him. How can it be that he is dead?

DISCIPLE 2:   I know I should not say this, but why did God let this happen? He loved God and I thought God loved him.

JESUS: *(Greets them from behind)* Good evening, gentlemen. You seem to be in a deep discussion about something. What are you so concerned about?

DISCIPLE 2:   You don't know? You must be the only person in Jerusalem who hasn't heard about the terrible things that happened there last week.

JESUS: What things?

DISCIPLE 1:   The things that happened to Jesus, the man from Nazareth. He was a prophet who did incredible miracles. he cured the blind, healed the mute, raised the widow's son from the dead. He fed multitudes of people with only five loaves of bread and two fish.

DISCIPLE 2:   He was a mighty teacher, highly regarded by both God and man. He taught us about good and evil, about salvation, righteousness, forgiveness and about God's love for us. But the chief priests and our religious leaders arrested him and handed him over to the Roman government to be condemned to death, and they crucified him.

DISCIPLE 1:   This morning some women from the group of his followers were at his tomb and came back with an amazing report that his body was missing. They had seen an angel who told them that Jesus is alive. Some of our men went out to see, and sure enough, Jesus' body was gone, just as the women had said.

But he can't be alive. We saw the nails driven through his hands. We saw his blood dripping to the ground. We heard him cry out in anguish to God.

DISCIPLE 2: We saw him take his last breath. We saw Joseph take his body down and place it in the tomb wrapped in the burial cloths.

JESUS: You are such foolish, foolish people! You find it so hard to believe all that the prophets wrote in the scriptures, even after he had explained it to you. Wasn't it clearly predicted by the prophets that the Messiah would have to suffer all these things before entering his time of glory? Didn't Jesus tell you that he came from the Father into the world and that he would be leaving the world going to the Father? He said, "A little while and you will no longer see me and again a little while and you will see me." Remember?

DISCIPLE 1: Yes, but we didn't understand that. There were many things we didn't understand.

JESUS: He said, "You have pain now, but I will see you again and your hearts will rejoice and no one will take your joy from you." Listen, I will tell you more. *(He pantomimes talking to them as Congregation sings Hymn: "ON THE DAY OF RESURRECTION")*

DISCIPLE 2: You have made it all to clear to us. I remember he did tell us these things. Come, visit with us. Stay the night and rest.

JESUS: Thank you. I will join you for a little while.
(The hymn tune is played while they take seats at a table. Jesus lifts the cup.)

JESUS: Take this and share it among yourselves. For I will not drink wine again until the Kingdom of God has come. *(They drink from the cup.)*

DISCIPLE 2: He speaks strangely. What does this mean?

JESUS: This is my body given for you. Eat it in remembrance of me. *(He backs off into an unseen areas as they eat the bread.)*

DISCIPLE 1: I have heard this before. This is Jesus. He is alive!

DISCIPLE 1: He is gone!

DISCIPLE 2: We must go back, immediately and tell the others that he lives. Jesus lives!

(Congregation sings "He Lives" as disciples go into the congregation.)

DISCIPLES: He lives! He Lives! He Lives! *(They exit still shouting)*

LOOKING FOR JESUS

This presentation may be given during the Easter or Pentecost season

(One woman enters, kneels and prays. The first seven CHILDREN enter).

PERSON 1:   Excuse me, miss. We're looking for Jesus. We were told that he would be here. We want to see him and thank him for all that he has done for us. Can you tell us where we can find him?

WOMAN: He now sits at the right hand of God but his spirit is always with us.

PERSON 2:   We have heard so many wonderful things about him. We never met him in person but we learned about him from our parents, and from our ministers and Sunday School teachers at church and we have read his words in the Bible.

PERSON 4:   I know that Jesus loved little children. He told the disciples to let the children come to him for theirs is the kingdom of heaven. That's why I am here.

PERSON 5:   Whenever I feel bad or unhappy I remind myself *(SINGS)* "Jesus loves me this I know for the Bible tells me so. Little ones to him belong. They are weak but he is strong. Yes, Jesus loves me. Yes, Jesus loves me. Yes, Jesus loves me for the Bible tells me so." Then I feel better. I want to tell him that.

PERSON 6:   Sometimes when I am afraid or someone is threatening to hurt me, I remember that Jesus said, "I am with you always!" I keep saying it until I start feeling better and then I'm not afraid of anything or anybody. I know he's with me.

PERSON 7:   My Sunday School teacher told me that if I want Jesus to do things for me, I should do good for others. And the first thing I should do is forgive people when they do mean things. That's not always easy to do. Sometimes I just want to bop them with my fist. But Jesus doesn't bop me when I do wrong. He forgives me so I try to do the same. I want to tell him I'm trying.

(Persons 8 - 12 are younger children. They enter)

PERSON 8:   Jesus told his disciples "Feed my sheep" He was talking about the people who had no food to eat. We are his disciples now and it is up to us to feed his sheep. I want to do my part.

PERSON 9:   He told us to pray a lot—all during the day. Then we can understand him better and trust him more.

PERSON 10:   Jesus said "Do good to those who hate you." That's not easy!

PERSON 11:   He said "Give and you will receive."

PERSON 12:   He said "Treat others as you want them to treat you."

PERSON 13:   There is so much we have learned from Jesus. If we could only tell him how much we love him.

PERSON 14:   We can tell him. Every time something good happens to us, we can say to ourselves "Thank you, Jesus" and he will hear us.

PERSON 1:   And Jesus said if we can't remember all of the commandments, to remember the most important ones, to love God with all your heart, soul, and mind, and love your neighbor as yourself. If I love everybody, forgive them, help them, and I love myself, then God will know I love him.

WOMAN: I have heard all that you have to say about Jesus. You asked me where to find him. You have already found him. He is in your heart and he has heard you. For he is with us in spirit. Let us rejoice and praise God for giving us this day and everyday to celebrate his Resurrection! Spread the word to others, tell them the good news that Jesus Christ is with us today and every day.

             (CAST AND CONGREGATION sing "Surely the Presence Of The Lord")

Other suggested hymns include "I'm Goin'a Sing When The Spirit Says Sing" and "Sweet Sweet Spirit"

DEDICATION OF THE TEMPLE

2 Chronicles 5-7

(CHORUS stands in the center. VOICES 1&2, SOLOMON and instrumentalists are a part of the CHORUS. Trumpet or organ plays a fanfare.)

VOICE 1:   The temple was finally finished. The workers, thousands of them looked up at their handiwork. It was great in size for Solomon knew that thousands of people would be coming for the festivals and for daily sacrifices. He had sent for a skilled artist, who had sculptured cherubims overlaid in gold to hang over the Holy Place. The ark had been carefully brought in and placed and all of the holy vessels of David's father were brought there.

VOICE 2:   And on the day of the dedication, thousands of people from all the Levitical tribes congregated, just like you here today, full of joy and thanksgiving while the priests went into the Holy place to sanctify themselves.

(CHORUS speaks each phrase higher in pitch and louder.)

CHORUS: Outside, all of us, the musicians and our friends and families dressed in fine linens, waited with our cymbals, harps and lyres and stood east of the altar with the 120 priests who were trumpeters. It was our joy to make ourselves heard in unison, in praise and thanksgiving to the Lord.

(Drum roll begins softly)

VOICE 1:   Then the priests came out and we raised our song with voices and instruments. *(Cymbals clash, instruments and singers perform in unison.)*

CHORUS: "God is good for his steadfast love endures forever" *(3 times)*

(CHORUS speaks each line higher in pitch and louder.)

CHORUS: And just at that moment, the glory of the Lord, came as a bright cloud and filled the Temple so that the priests could not continue their work. Our hearts were filled with the Holy Spirit and we began to sing again.

"God is good for his steadfast love endures forever" *(3 times)*

VOICE 2: Then Solomon prayed. *(SOLOMON kneels)*

(Hymn tune "O Love That Will Not Let Me Go" is played by a single instrument during prayer.)

SOLOMON: O Lord God of Israel, there is no God like you in all of heaven and earth. You are the God who keeps his kind promises to all those who obey you, and who are anxious to do your will. You have said that you would live in the thick darkness, but I have made a Temple for you, O Lord, to live in forever knowing that even the heaven and the heaven of heavens cannot contain you, how much less this Temple which I have built. I ask you now to look down with favor day and night upon this Temple—upon this place where you have said that you would put your name. May you always hear and answer the prayers I will pray to you as I face toward this place. And hear the prayers of all of your people when they pray in this Temple; and when you hear us, Lord, forgive us.

(CHORUS speaks each sentence higher in pitch and louder.)

VOICE 1: As he finished praying, fire flashed down from heaven and burned up the sacrifices!

And the glory of the Lord filled the Temple, so that the priests could not enter.

And all of us who had been a part of it, worshiped and thanked the Lord.

Music